Old English Sheepdogs

by Julie Murray

Abdo Kids Jumbo is an Imprint of Abdo Kids
abdobooks.com

abdobooks.com

Published by Abdo Kids, a division of ABDO, P.O. Box 398166, Minneapolis, Minnesota 55439.

Printed in the United States of America, North Mankato, Minnesota.

102023

012024

THIS BOOK CONTAINS
RECYCLED MATERIALS

Photo Credits: Alamy, Getty Images, Shutterstock, Thinkstock

Production Contributors: Teddy Borth, Jennie Forsberg, Grace Hansen
Design Contributors: Candice Keimig, Pakou Moua

Library of Congress Control Number: 2023937686

Publisher's Cataloging-in-Publication Data

Names: Murray, Julie, author.

Title: Old English sheepdogs / by Julie Murray

Description: Minneapolis, Minnesota : Abdo Kids, 2024 | Series: Dogs | Includes online resources and index.

Identifiers: ISBN 9781098268534 (lib. bdg.) | ISBN 9781098269234 (ebook) | ISBN 9781098269586 (Read-to-Me ebook)

Subjects: LCSH: Old English sheepdog--Juvenile literature. | Sheep dogs--Juvenile literature. | Dogs--Juvenile literature. | Dogs--Behavior--Juvenile literature. | Animal behavior--Juvenile literature.

Classification: DDC 599.772--dc23

Table of Contents

Old English Sheepdogs 4

Grooming 14

Exercise. 16

Personality 18

More Facts 22

Glossary 23

Index 24

Abdo Kids Code. 24

Old English Sheepdogs

Old English sheepdogs can be traced back to the early 1800s. They were bred in western England to herd sheep and cattle.

England
Europe

Old English sheepdogs were **drover** dogs. They herded sheep over long distances on their way to market. The dogs moved the sheep during the day. At night, they stood guard.

Old English sheepdogs have muscular bodies and strong legs. They can be 22 inches (55.9 cm) tall and weigh 100 pounds (45.4 kg).

An Old English sheepdog's coat is soft and long. The coat can be a mix of colors. It can be shades of blue, gray, **grizzle**, blue **merle**, and white.

Old English sheepdogs have a double coat. The outer coat is waterproof. The **undercoat** is thick. It keeps them warm in cold temperatures.

Grooming

Old English sheepdogs need a lot of grooming. They are known to **shed** a lot! Daily brushing will keep their coat from getting **matted**.

Exercise

Old English sheepdogs are playful and energetic. They need daily exercise. They love to run and play with their owners.

Personality

Old English sheepdogs are very smart. They can be goofy at times. They can also be **stubborn**. Proper training is needed.

Old English sheepdogs make great family pets. They like children and other animals. They do not like to be left alone for long periods of time. Being around others helps them be their happiest!

More Facts

- Old English sheepdogs can grow their hair so long that it covers their entire face, including their eyes!

- They are often called "Bobtails." This is because the dogs can be born with a **bobtail**. It was also common for the tail to be **docked** at an early age.

- Old English sheepdogs were recognized by the American Kennel Club in 1888. They are members of the Herding Group.

Glossary

bobtail – an animal tail that is naturally short.

docked – to have cut part of an animal's tail short.

drover – someone who drives animals, especially sheep or cattle, to a place where they can be sold.

grizzle – a mix of colors with no obvious pattern.

matted – tangled into a thick mass.

merle – irregular patches of color.

shed – to give off hair.

stubborn – not willing to accept control.

undercoat – the short hairs growing close to an animal's skin, covered by longer hair or fur.

Index

body 8

coat 10, 12, 14

color 10

England 4

exercise 16

grooming 14

guarding 6

herding 4, 6

history 4, 6

intelligence 18

legs 8

personality 16, 18, 20

size 8

training 18